ROSEN Verified
THE BILL OF RIGHTS

What Is Free Speech?

Jill Keppeler

ROSEN PUBLISHING

Published in 2024 by The Rosen Publishing Group, Inc.
2544 Clinton Street, Buffalo, NY 14224

First Edition

Editor: Greg Roza
Book Design: Michael Flynn

Photo Credits: Cover, p. 21 DC_Studio/Shutterstock.com; (series background) PinkPueblo/Shutterstock.com; p. 5 wellphoto/Shutterstock.com; p. 7 Sean Pavone/Shutterstock.com; p. 8 Janusz Pienkowski/Shutterstock.com; p. 9 zimmytws/Shutterstock.com; p. 11 https://commons.wikimedia.org/wiki/File:Pictures_of_English_History_Plate_XXIV_-_King_John_and_Magna_Carta.jpg; p. 13 Dmitrii Sakharov/Shutterstock.com; p. 15 Claudine Van Massenhove/Shutterstock.com; p. 17 Ted Pendergast/Shutterstock.com; p. 19 Monkey Business Images/Shutterstock.com; p. 23 PR Image Factory/Shutterstock.com; p. 25 Fizkes/Shutterstock.com; p. 27 wellphoto/Shutterstock.com; p. 29 courtsey of the Library of Congress; p. 31 Glynnis Jones/Shutterstock.com; p. 33 Chayantorn Tongmorn/Shutterstock.com; p. 35 Justin Berken/Shutterstock.com; p. 37 Rawpixel.com/Shutterstock.com; p. 39 FUN FUN PHOTO/Shutterstock.com; p. 41 Prostock-studio/Shutterstock.com; p. 43 DGLimages/Shutterstock.com.

Cataloging-in-Publication Data

Names: Keppeler, Jill.
Title: What is free speech? / Jill Keppeler.
Description: New York : Rosen Publishing, 2024. | Series: Rosen verified: the Bill of Rights | Includes glossary and index.
Identifiers: ISBN 9781499469639 (pbk.) | ISBN 9781499469646 (library bound) | ISBN 9781499469653 (ebook)
Subjects: LCSH: Freedom of speech--United States--Juvenile literature.
Classification: LCC KF4772.K47 2024 | DDC 342.7308'53--dc23

Manufactured in the United States of America

CONTENTS

Freedom of Speech and More

In the United States, we have freedom of speech. But what does that mean? Does it mean you can say anything you want and never get in trouble? What promises us that freedom? What other freedoms do we have? These are important questions.

The First Amendment, or change, to the U.S. **Constitution** promises the freedom of speech. It also promises other freedoms, including freedom of the press and freedom of **religion**. While these freedoms are key to our **democracy**, many people don't have a clear idea of what they include—or what they don't include. There are limits to them. However, everyone in the country, including kids, has these freedoms.

What would you use your First Amendment rights to say here?

Does that mean you can call people mean names in school and get away with it? Nope! Your parent probably couldn't call their boss a name and still keep their job either. So, what good is the First Amendment? Well, it **protects** us from the government arresting us for our speech or trying to take away those other freedoms. This includes the federal, or national, government, state governments, and local governments. It includes all branches of government too. Read on to learn more.

The Bill of Rights

In 1787, many **representatives** from most of the U.S. states arrived in Philadelphia, Pennsylvania. They meant to change the first constitution they had created. The group soon decided the country needed a whole new constitution instead.

After much talking and arguing, the group came up with a new law of the land for the country. However, some representatives still didn't like it. They said the constitution needed a bill of rights. This is a list of individual rights and limits on government.

GEORGE MASON

George Mason (1725–1792) was a representative from Virginia who took part in creating the U.S. Constitution. Before that, he wrote the Virginia Declaration of Rights. When the time came to OK the U.S. Constitution, Mason wouldn't do it. He wanted a bill of rights. He also didn't like the power it gave the federal government.

The representatives met in the Pennsylvania State House. It's now called Independence Hall.

THE ARTICLES OF CONFEDERATION

The Articles of Confederation was the first constitution of the United States. It went into effect in 1781. This constitution gave little power to the federal government. In time, the government was so weak it caused problems. That's when representatives met in 1787 to change things.

Key Changes

Nine of the 13 states needed to ratify, or approve, the U.S. Constitution. Some would only do this if a bill of rights was added. Representatives promised to do this. In June 1788, New Hampshire became the ninth state to ratify the Constitution and it became law.

Representative James Madison presented a list of amendments to Congress in 1789. A few months later, Congress sent 12 of these amendments to the states to be ratified. In time, 10 amendments were approved. The U.S. Bill of Rights was officially law.

JAMES MADISON

James Madison (1751–1836) was a representative from Virginia. He played a big part in creating the U.S. Constitution. He was also the main author of the Bill of Rights. He would later become the fourth president of the United States.

BILL OF RIGHTS TIMELINE

May to September 1787	The Constitutional **Convention** meets in Philadelphia.
September 1787	The Constitutional Convention sends the new constitution to the states.
June 1788	The ninth state (New Hampshire) ratifies the new U.S. Constitution.
June 1789	James Madison presents a list of amendments to Congress.
October 1789	Congress sends 12 amendments to the states.
December 1791	Three-fourths of the states have ratified 10 amendments, creating the new Bill of Rights.

The First Amendment is the top amendment in the Bill of Rights.

Origins

The rights promised in the First Amendment came from many sources. One is the Magna Carta. Nobles in England forced King John to sign it in 1215. This **document** includes the idea that no one is above the law. This even includes the king.

In 1641, during the early days of British colonies in North America, the Massachusetts Bay Colony adopted an early list of individual liberties. This included the right to **petition**. Another **inspiration** was the writing of John Locke.

JOHN LOCKE

John Locke (1632–1704) was an English **philosopher**. His works led to the U.S. Constitution as well as the amendments of the Bill of Rights. He wrote that all people are born with certain rights. These rights, Locke said, can never be taken away.

EVEN EARLIER ORIGINS

Long before the Magna Carta, the ancient Greeks valued the ideal of freedom of speech. They used the word "parrhesia," which means "to speak freely." It was an important part of democracy in Athens.

The Magna Carta also listed individual liberties. It included many fixes in local government.

Five Freedoms

The First Amendment says: "Congress shall make no law respecting an establishment of religion, or prohibiting (banning) the free exercise thereof; or abridging (lessening) the freedom of speech, or of the press; or the right of the people peaceably to assemble (to gather in one place), and to petition the Government for a redress (correction) of grievances (problems)."

These words cover five freedoms. The most famous is probably the freedom of speech. However, the others are very important too.

THE FIRST FIRST AMENDMENT

Madison's version, or form, of the First Amendment was more than twice as long as the version in the Constitution. It **described** the rights more. However, it meant much the same thing as the final one.

VERIFIED

The National Constitution Center is in Philadelphia. It also has a website. Its goal is to teach people about the U.S. Constitution. Find out more at **constitutioncenter.org.**

The National Constitution Center, shown here, isn't home to the original constitution. That's in the National **Archives** in Washington, D.C.

No State Religion

The first clause, or part, of the First Amendment is called the establishment clause. It says that Congress can make no laws about "an establishment of religion." This means the government can't name an official religion. It's also not supposed to favor one religion over others. It can't force anyone to take part in a religion.

Many people say the establishment clause means that there should be separation between church and state. However, different courts have looked at this very differently.

THE LEMON TEST

The Supreme Court case *Lemon v. Kurtzman* was decided in 1971. It created a test with three questions. They're meant for figuring out if a government act goes against the establishment clause.

DOES THE ACT:

- Have a nonreligious purpose
- Not advance or favor a set of religious beliefs
- Not overly **involve** the government with religion

VERIFIED

The U.S. Supreme Court is the highest court in the country. It sometimes has to interpret, or explain the meaning of, laws. This includes the U.S. Constitution and amendments. For more information on the Supreme Court, visit **supremecourt.gov**.

This tower is all that remains of one of the earliest church buildings in the original 13 colonies. It was built in the 1600s in Jamestown Colony.

The Free Exercise Thereof

The second clause of the First Amendment is related to the first clause. It says the government can't limit the "free exercise" of religion. This means it can't treat people badly because of their religion. It can't **discriminate** against people who practice a certain religion. It also includes the freedom to take part in most religious **rituals.**

Sometimes these clauses seem to work against each other. They're meant to balance each other out. If the government goes too far on one, it can be limited by the other.

THE HISTORY BEHIND

There's a lot of history behind these clauses. People seeking religious freedom founded some of the 13 colonies. In Europe, many people were treated badly for following a different religion. They didn't want that in the new country.

CLAUSE VS. CLAUSE

The clauses meet in the case of military chaplains. A chaplain is a religious leader for a military group. The government creates and pays for chaplain programs. This seems like it's against the establishment clause. However, many military members couldn't freely exercise their religion if the government didn't do this.

An Army National Guard chaplain leads a prayer during a Veterans Day event. The Supreme Court has said military chaplain programs don't go against the First Amendment.

Speaking Freely

The next clause is the one the First Amendment is most known for. It says the government can't abridge, or lessen, the freedom of speech. It can't say that people in the United States can't talk about certain opinions. This is even true if those opinions are against the government.

This freedom of speech doesn't just cover **politics.** It also covers subjects such as religion and science. However, there are some limits. And there can be some **consequences.**

STUDENTS' RIGHTS

According to the ACLU, in a public school, you have the right to speak out about your views. You have the right to hand out petitions. You have the right to wear shirts and clothing that share your opinion. You don't have the right to be disruptive. This means you can't get in the way of the school's purpose of education.

VERIFIED

The American Civil Liberties Union (ACLU) was founded in 1920. It works to protect people's rights as promised in the Constitution and Bill of Rights. For more information, visit **aclu.org**. The ACLU offers advice for students on their rights too. Visit **www.aclu.org/know-your-rights/students-rights**.

In a public school, your school staff disagreeing with your opinion isn't enough to make your speech disruptive.

Sorts of Speech

Different types of speech fall under the protection of the First Amendment. There are also a few types of speech that don't. Protected speech can include political speech or religious speech. It can include speech about morals and speech about social issues. It can also include gossip. This means stories about the personal lives of other people.

Even hate speech may be protected if it doesn't include a threat, or promise of harm. So is speech that might offend, or upset, people.

COMMERCIAL SPEECH

The word "commercial" has to do with buying and selling. Commercial speech is speech related to this. This includes **advertisements**. There are some protections for commercial speech. However, the government can make laws banning false ads and limiting other ones.

HATE SPEECH

Hate speech is public speech that expresses, or makes known, hate toward other people.

- This may include individuals or groups.
- It can be words or pictures. It can also be gestures, or body movements.
- It discriminates against people. Or it is pejorative. This means that it's rude or offensive.
- It calls out things (real or imagined) about the individual or group.

Art is a type of speech. The ACLU works to support free expression through art too.

Limits

The free speech clause doesn't cover everything. The government can make rules about the time and place of speech. For example, it can say that a **protest** can't block cars in a busy area.

Some types of speech can be limited. This includes threats and so-called "fighting words." This is speech meant to cause a physical, or bodily, fight. Another kind of limited speech is incitement. This means speech that's trying to get people to break laws right then.

OTHER UNPROTECTED SPEECH

Defamation is also not protected by the First Amendment. This means false speech that's trying to get people to think badly of someone or something. This is called "libel" when it's in print. It's called "slander" when spoken.

WHAT'S OBSCENITY?

Obscenity means something that goes far against the public sense of decency. This means what's right and moral. People can have a very different sense of what's obscene! Obscenity is not protected by the First Amendment. However, the legal, or law-related, idea of obscenity is very narrow.

Fraud also isn't protected by the First Amendment. Fraud is using lies to take something from another person.

Consequences

There's one important thing many people don't understand about the First Amendment. Freedom of speech doesn't mean freedom from consequences. The First Amendment just protects people from being arrested by the government for their speech. Other people or groups can still act against them.

This could even apply to you and your friends. It could include a group turning away from another person if they think their opinions are awful. It could also mean a private business firing a worker for their speech.

IN SOME CASES

Sometimes, laws do protect people in the case of private groups or businesses. One is the Civil Rights Act of 1964. It says private businesses can't discriminate because of religion. Race, color, sex, and national origin are also protected.

SILENT SPEAKING

Sometimes, actions can also be speech. They can be symbolic, or meaning something without using words. This includes burning the U.S. flag. In *Texas v. Johnson* in 1989, the Supreme Court said this is protected speech.

If you and your friend group don't like what another friend says and stop talking to them, that's not against the First Amendment. Those are consequences for their speech!

Powers of the Press

Freedom of the press is the next part of the First Amendment. It's key to democracy. It allows the news media to report on what the government is doing without being silenced. James Madison called the press "one of the great bulwarks (protectors) of liberty." This was in his original First Amendment.

The news media is supposed to keep the government **accountable** to the people. Press freedom is based on the people's right to know what their leaders are doing.

SHIELD LAWS

Most states have media shield laws. These are laws that give news reporters some rights to refuse to tell the government where they got certain information. It also includes the information itself. There is no federal shield law.

VERIFIED

The Freedom of the Press Foundation protects and defends, or stands up for, journalism. This is the job of collecting, writing, and editing news stories for newspapers and other media. To learn more, visit **freedom.press**. The foundation also tracks press freedom problems in the United States. Find the press freedom tracker at **pressfreedomtracker.us**.

Shield laws may give reporters absolute, or full, protection. Or they may give qualified, or limited, protection. Sometimes reporters will even go to jail to protect their sources.

The Best Defense

In 1735, John Peter Zenger was charged with libel in the New York colony. Zenger printed a newspaper. He said things about Governor William Cosby there. The governor didn't like this at all. He tried to shut it down.

Zenger's lawyer told the court that Zenger did print things about Cosby. He then said that Cosby had to prove they weren't true. The jury was just supposed to decide if Zenger printed the words. Instead, it said Zenger wasn't guilty.

"The question before the court and you, gentlemen of the jury, is not of small or private concern. It is not the cause of one poor printer, nor of New York alone, which you are now trying. No! It may in its consequence affect every free man that lives under a British government on the main of America. It is the best case. It is the cause of liberty."

—Lawyer Andrew Hamilton's words to the Zenger jury

FAST FACT

The Zenger case led to the idea that truth is the best **defense** against libel charges. This is still true.

The Zenger case took place before the colonies became a country. Truth as a defense against libel was a new idea at the time. It later became a key part of U.S. free speech law.

Prior Restraint

Many U.S. court cases have been about press freedoms. The *Near v. Minnesota* Supreme Court case in 1931 was important. The court found that prior restraint goes against the First Amendment. Prior restraint is when a government keeps a news story from being printed.

In 1971, the court revisited this idea in *New York Times v. United States*. This case was about the Pentagon Papers. These papers were about the origin of the Vietnam War. The government didn't want them printed. However, the *Times* won.

VERIFIED

The *New York Times* has millions of print and digital readers. It's based in New York City. For more information, visit **www.nytimes.com**.

MAJOR FREEDOM OF THE PRESS CASES

1735	*Rex v. Zenger*	Establishes truth as best defense against libel charges.
1931	*Near v. Minnesota*	Says that prior restraint goes against the First Amendment.
1964	*New York Times v. Sullivan*	Protects statements against public officials unless the speaker lied while meaning to defame. The statement must have been made with "actual malice" This means knowing it was wrong.
1971	*New York Times v. United States*	This is the Pentagon Papers case.

The *New York Times* was founded in 1851. It's won 132 Pulitzer Prizes. This is more than any other newspaper.

Student Journalists

Young people also have First Amendment rights. But the rules for student journalists may be more limited. This was part of the 1988 Supreme Court case *Hazelwood School District v. Kuhlmeier*.

In this case, a principal tried to bar two stories from a high school newspaper. The court said that schools can set a higher standard for student newspapers. They can restrict, or limit, their content. This is if the content is against the school's mission, or job.

TINKER V. DES MOINES

Tinker v. Des Moines was a Supreme Court case in 1969. A few students were sent home from school for wearing black armbands. They were protesting the Vietnam War. The court ruled in favor of the students. It said students don't leave their right to freedom of speech "at the schoolhouse gate."

VERIFIED
The Student Press Law Center works for the rights of high school and college journalists. For more information, visit **splc.org**.

Student journalists do have some freedoms. Their school must have a good reason if it wants to limit what they print. Some states give student journalists more freedoms too.

Peaceably to Assemble

The next part of the First Amendment protects “the right of the people peaceably to assemble.” This is the right of people to gather and share and express ideas. It’s considered just as important as the freedoms of speech and the press. It includes peaceful protests and meetings.

There are some limits, as with the other clauses. People can’t meet while meaning to disturb, or upset, the public peace. Every state has different laws about what this means.

THE FOURTEENTH AMENDMENT

This amendment, added in 1868, affects the First Amendment. One part says that states can’t make or enforce, or carry out, laws that take away people’s rights “without due process of law.” The Supreme Court used this to apply all the amendments to the states and local governments.

DISTURBING THE PEACE

In general, disturbing the peace means:

- Making too much noise
- Encouraging, or supporting, violence, or harm
- Blocking a public space for too long

You have the right to speak out when in public areas. But you can't block other people from going somewhere. Protests that include closing streets or public areas for a time might need a permit.

Freedom of Association

Part of the right to assemble is the freedom of association. This means that people are free to associate, or be with, other people of their choice. This may include political parties. It may also include other groups with a certain message.

People have privacy of membership rights too. Groups don't usually have to tell the government who their members are. Groups also have the right to keep people from joining if those people may go against the group's speech.

GENDER DISCRIMINATION

Roberts v. United States Jaycees took place in 1984. The Supreme Court said that groups can't keep people out just because of their sex. It's only allowed as a reason if it would change the group's message.

UNION ISSUES

These rules affect **labor unions**. The freedom of association includes the right to associate. It also includes the right not to associate. In 1977, the Supreme Court said unions can't make public employees pay some fees. In 2018, the court made that rule stronger.

The Equal Access Act was passed in 1984. It says public schools can't accept federal money if they break certain rules. They must give students their right to have meetings.

Right to Petition

The last clause of the First Amendment says people have the right to "petition the government for a redress of grievances." This means they can ask the government to fix things that are wrong. This can include public protesting. It can include filing a lawsuit. It can also include testifying, or speaking, before a government group.

Today, this right can include signing a petition online. It can include emailing a government official. There are more ways than ever to use this right.

> "We have Petitioned for Redress in the most **humble** terms: Our repeated Petitions have been answered only by repeated **injury**."
>
> **—The Declaration of Independence, 1776**

IN THE BEGINNING

The right to petition is part of the beginning of the United States. In the 1700s, the British colonies in North America sent petitions to King George III asking him to change things. This included the Olive Branch petition of 1775. The king wouldn't even read it. This set the colonies on the road to war.

Speaking at a public school board meeting can be exercising your right to petition.

Not only was the right to petition key to the beginning of the United States, it's been important throughout its history. Thousands of people petitioned for the end of slavery in the early years of the country. Even people who couldn't vote (such as women and enslaved people) could petition. And they did.

Many social movements were possible because of this right. This includes the abolition, or end of slavery, movement. It includes the fight for women's voting rights. It was a huge part of the civil rights movement.

THE GAG RULE

In the 1830s, the number of antislavery petitions grew. By 1836, the House of Representatives had had enough. It adopted the "gag rule." This said that more petitions wouldn't be dealt with. Former president John Quincy Adams fought this. He even read petitions from enslaved people on the House floor. In 1844, the House finally decided the rule was unconstitutional.

LOBBYING

The right to petition includes the right to lobby government officials. This means to try to get them to make decisions for or against something. It can include individuals or private interest groups. Some groups hire full-time lobbyists.

Today, the right to petition is often more limited. It doesn't mean that a petition will be answered. It means that people can complain to the government without being **punished**.

Social Media

The Bill of Rights was written hundreds of years before social media arrived. We can't know what the founders would have thought about it! Still, the First Amendment deals with social media too. It can be **complicated**. Government can generally only control things on social media that it also could control in other media.

Social media companies are private businesses. They can decide what they allow. Some people think this should change. They say social media works as a public forum, or area.

Social media "websites can provide perhaps the most powerful mechanisms (ways) available to a private citizen to make his or her voice heard."

—The Supreme Court in *Packingham v. North Carolina* (2017)

SCHOOLS AND SOCIAL MEDIA

A public school probably can't punish you for things you post from somewhere else. That's only if those things don't have anything to do with school, though. The rules about disruption apply here too. Your posts can't be disruptive to education.

A post to social media that isn't made from school or on school time may be protected. Still, be careful.

Your Rights

As the United States moves further into the 21st century, new court cases and other changes will probably affect what the First Amendment means even more. We have more ways to speak our mind than ever before. Some people will try to control this. But others will work to be sure people can still protest and say what they think.

Young people have rights too. It's important to remember this. While you don't have the right to vote before you're 18, you can make your voice heard in other ways. You can speak at public meetings. You can write to your local newspaper or news website. You can create artwork that shows what you think. You may be able to go to a protest or another speech event. You can form clubs or other groups. You can start a school newspaper.

The ACLU says that the freedom to read is the freedom to think. It's important!

Stand up for what you believe in! That's the only way things will ever get better. Things that take away your freedoms are growing in some ways. For example, since 2021, some people are trying to ban books more and more often in schools. This is often because they don't want young people learning about some things. If you don't agree, speak up!

GLOSSARY

accountable: Responsible for giving an account of one's acts.

advertisement: Something shown to the public to try to sell something.

archive: A place where records are stored.

complicated: Hard to explain or understand, having many parts.

consequence: Something that happens because of a certain action or set of conditions.

constitution: The basic laws by which a country, state, or group is governed.

convention: A gathering of people who have a common interest or purpose.

defense: A way of guarding against something.

democracy: A government elected by the people, directly or indirectly.

describe: To tell someone what something is like.

discriminate: To treat people unequally based on class, race, religion, or other factors.

document: A formal piece of writing.

humble: Modest or meek in spirit or manner.

injury: Hurt, damage, or loss.

inspiration: The act or power of moving the mind or the emotions of others.

involve: To have or include someone or something as a part of something.

labor union: An organization of workers formed to protect the rights and advance the interests of its members concerning wages, benefits, and working conditions.

petition: To make a request. Or, a formal written request to a leader or government regarding a particular cause.

philosopher: A person who studies philosophy, or the study of the basic ideas about knowledge, right and wrong, reasoning, and the value of things.

politics: The activities of the government and government officials.

protect: To keep safe.

protest: An event at which a group objects to an idea, an act, or a way of doing something; to strongly oppose something.

punish: To cause to experience pain or suffering for having done wrong.

religion: A belief in and way of honoring a god or gods.

representative: Someone who acts officially for someone or something.

ritual: A religious ceremony, especially one consisting of a series of actions performed in a certain order.

INDEX